LUNCHEONETTE

LUNCHEONETTE

Ice-Cream, Beverage, and Sandwich Recipes from the Golden Age of the Soda Fountain

Illustrations by Carol Vidinghoff
Edited by Patricia M. Kelly

Crown Publishers, Inc.   New York

Portions of this book were previously published in
Soda Fountain and Luncheonette Drinks and Recipes by Louis DeGouy.

Illustrations copyright © 1989 by Carol Vidinghoff
Introductory remarks copyright © 1989 by Patricia M. Kelly

Published by Crown Publishers, Inc., 201 East 50th Street
New York, New York 10022
CROWN is a trademark of Crown Publishers, Inc.

Manufactured in Hong Kong

Library of Congress Cataloging-in-Publication Data

Luncheonette / edited by Patricia M. Kelly.
p. cm.
1. Sandwiches.   2. Ice cream, ices, etc.
3. Restaurants, lunch rooms, etc. — United States.
I. Kelly, Patricia M., 1958–
TX818.L86   1989
641.8′4 — dc20   89-7701

ISBN: 0-517-57297-4

Book design by Nancy Kenmore

10 9 8 7 6 5 4 3 2 1

First Edition

CONTENTS

*L*ouis P. DeGouy, *author* *of* Soda Fountain and Luncheonette Drinks and Recipes.

INTRODUCTION

To preserve your health during the warm season,
drink from two to five glasses of Dow's
Ice Cream Soda Water daily.

Advertisement for G. D. Dow's Drugstore, 1861

The happy marriage of soda fountain and drugstore began in 1825 in Philadelphia when Elias Durand began selling soda water in his drugstore as a simple remedy for an assortment of ailments from obesity and gout to dyspepsia. From that time right through the 1950s, drugstore soda fountains were places where women could go unescorted, courting couples sip sodas, men discuss world affairs, and everyone could obtain simple remedies such as fizz water (Alka Seltzer) or a C.O. cocktail (castor oil and soda) as well as sodas, malts, milk shakes, and eggnogs.

In addition to providing conversation and remedies, the soda fountain produced a new American hero in the person of the soda jerk. He (and it was almost always he) was a performer with an audience, a routine, and a unique dialogue. The *New York Times Magazine* for July 16, 1939, described soda jerks in this fashion:

> 90% of them are native Americans for the simple reason that, aside from the ability to break and drain an egg with one hand, carve chicken, butter toast, remember orders, and pull the proper faucets, the prime requisite of their station is the ability to bandy words.

"Adam and Eve on a Raft" (poached eggs on toast), "Twist It, Choke It, and Make It Cackle" (malted milk with an egg), and "Pig Between Two Sheets" (ham sandwich) were only a few of the common soda fountain calls that provided both entertainment for the audience and a memory aid for the soda jerk.

Although the drugstore soda fountain was an entertainment and social center for customers, it was also a source of profit for the proprietor. In the 1930s and '40s three quarters of all drugstores had soda fountains and these fountains were selling 30 percent of all of the ice cream sold in this country. Every third drugstore customer was a soda fountain customer. The Ice Cream Institute ran a series of seminars called "sundae schools" to promote new products and marketing techniques; its laboratories continually created new syrups, sundaes, and sodas. Journals like the *Ice Cream Trade Journal* and *American Druggist* and books like Louis P. DeGouy's *Soda Fountain and Luncheonette Drinks and Recipes* (J. O. Dahl, 1940) gave advice on how to run the soda fountain and provided recipes for soda fountain concoctions.

DeGouy was a professional chef trained under Auguste Escoffier. Subsequently he was executive chef to the royalty of Austria and Belgium and cooked in some of Europe's and America's best restaurants. He was also a food editor for *Gourmet* magazine. All of this training he brought to bear in *Soda Fountain and Luncheonette Drinks and Recipes*. Using his recipes and text and Carol Vidinghoff's illustrations, we hope to introduce you to the soda fountain of the 1930s and '40s and thus enable you to savor the sundaes, sodas, sandwiches, and atmosphere of a different time.

ICE-CREAM PREPARATIONS

INGREDIENTS *and*
MEASUREMENTS

These recipes are only guidelines; change them as you will. Add more ice cream, less syrup, different nuts, marshmallow instead of whipped cream. Please yourself since, unlike the soda jerk of yesterday, you do not have to make the dish the exact same way each time. You will find most of the ingredients necessary to prepare soda fountain concoctions readily available in supermarkets and specialty food stores. Recipes are provided for difficult-to-find or unavailable items.

Ice-cream scoops come in a variety of sizes and shapes. Scoops are numbered according to the number of portions they will scoop from a quart of ice cream. For instance, a Number 24 scoop will yield 24 portions per quart of ice cream. Ladles are measured in ounces. Each ounce is equivalent to 2 tablespoons. A soda spoon holds about 1 teaspoon.

SODA FOUNTAIN
NECESSITIES

The well-stocked soda fountain of the 1930s and '40s contained — in addition to various flavors of ice cream — syrups, fruits, nuts, and miscellaneous items, depending on the size of the fountain and demand. These had to be "the highest quality syrups, crushed fruits, malted milk, chocolate and nuts [the proprietor could] buy" (*American Druggist*, 1937).

A dispenser need not prepare this many syrups. This would require an elaborate and costly organization. However, in case of emergency — for instance, in case of nondelivery — it is sometimes very useful to know how to prepare and combine simple and easy-to-make syrups which are so necessary for the success of a soda fountain.

Although many of these items are no longer used or available, the following will give you an idea of the ingredients commonly used to construct soda fountain concoctions.

Concentrated Syrups

Apple syrup
Applejack syrup
Apricot syrup
Banana syrup
Butterscotch
  syrup
Celery syrup

Chocolate syrup
Coca-Cola syrup
Coffee syrup
Lemon syrup
Lime syrup
Maple syrup
Orange syrup

Orgeat syrup
Peach syrup
Pineapple syrup
Raspberry syrup
Strawberry
  syrup
Vanilla syrup

Flavoring Extracts

Almond extract
Apple extract
Ginger extract
Maple extract

Nutmeg extract
Orange extract
Peach extract
Root beer extract

Spearmint
  extract
Walnut extract

Fruits

Bananas
Candied fruits
Cherries

Crushed
  peaches
Maraschino
  cherries

Pineapple sticks
Raspberries
Stewed figs
Strawberries

Nuts

Almonds
Brazil nuts
Cashews

Coconut
  (shredded)
Hazelnuts
Peanuts

Pecans
Pistachios
Walnuts

Miscellaneous Necessities

Assorted cookies
Bromo Seltzer
Chocolate shot
Coffee
Cream
Crème de
  menthe

Eggs
Grenadine
Kirsch
Malted milk
  powder
Marshmallow
  fluff

Milk
Mineral waters
Orange flower
  water
Parfait
Phosphate
  solution

Fresh, canned, preserved, and crushed fruits are probably the most valuable adjunct of the soda dispenser, and while all are used — fresh when in season, canned and preserved out of season — the fresh fruits are of especial value in developing the soda fountain trade. There is something about fresh fruit, a delicate flavor and peculiar freshness that cannot be compared against other fruits.

The use of different forms of dippers or cones, as well as different forms of cream, adds much to the serving of sundaes. A number of different scoops should be at the disposal of the dispenser.

Luncheonette

Dishes and Utensils

Banana split
  dishes
Glasses
Ladles

Pastry tube
Scoops, assorted
  sizes and
  shapes
Shakers, covered

Soda spoons
Soda straws
Sundae dishes
Toothpicks

SUNDAES

Perhaps the most popular of all soda fountain concoctions is the ice-cream sundae. The sundae was first served sometime in the late 1890s by a soda fountain proprietor who eliminated the soda water from an ice-cream soda to comply with the Blue Laws prohibiting the sale of sodas on the Sabbath. The sundae consists quite simply of ice cream, a dressing, and a garnish, but the variations on this theme are innumerable. Some of the sundaes of the 1930s and '40s were so complicated that the Ice Cream Institute issued diagrams with recipes for new sundaes. Use the following sundae recipes as a starting point for creating your own concoctions.

FEATURED FLAVOR

Delicious
STRAWBERRY SODA and SUNDAE

The best manager in the world cannot get along unless he has an organization that is pulling for him.

Bachelor Sundae

Vanilla ice cream
Chocolate ice cream
Raisin Cream Sauce (recipe, see page 30)

Hazelnut Cream Sauce (recipe, see page 30)
Cherries

Put I scoop of vanilla ice cream and I of chocolate ice cream on an oblong dish. Pour Raisin Cream Sauce over the vanilla, Hazelnut Cream Sauce over the chocolate, and top each with a cherry.

Black and White Sundae

Vanilla wafers
Vanilla ice cream
Chocolate ice cream
Whipped cream

Chocolate Marshmallow Sauce (recipe, see page 27)
Pecans, chopped
Walnuts, chopped

Place 4 vanilla wafers on a flat dish, forming two squares. On one of the squares put I scoop of vanilla ice cream, and on the other I scoop of chocolate ice cream. Ladle whipped cream over the vanilla ice cream and Chocolate Marshmallow Sauce over the chocolate. Put I soda spoon of chopped pecans at one end of the dish and I spoon of chopped walnuts at the other.

Boston Banana Sundae

Banana, split in half
  lengthwise
Coffee ice cream
Vanilla ice cream
Orange sherbet

Marshmallow Cream Sauce
  (recipe, see page 31)
Strawberries, crushed
Cherry
Whipped cream
Walnuts, finely chopped

Place the banana halves, cut side up, in a banana split dish. On one end, place I scoop of coffee ice cream; on the other, I scoop of vanilla ice cream. In the center put I small scoop of orange sherbet. Pour some Marshmallow Cream Sauce over the coffee ice cream, fresh crushed strawberries over the vanilla ice cream, and put a cherry atop the orange sherbet. Decorate with small puffs of whipped cream and dust with finely chopped walnuts.

Caramel Cream Sundae

Lettuce leaves
Chocolate ice cream
Vanilla ice cream

Strawberry ice cream
Caramel Cream Sauce
  (recipe, see page 30)
Whipped cream

Line a sundae dish with crisp lettuce leaves. Over the lettuce place I scoop each of chocolate, vanilla, and strawberry ice cream. Cover with hot Caramel Cream Sauce and whipped cream.

Although a sundae is supposed to be a cold, refreshing sweet and a cooler at the same time, certain sundaes may be served hot.

BANANA SKYSCRAPER

Cherry Chopped Suey Sundae

Candied cherries, chopped
Pineapple, crushed
Pistachio ice cream

Whipped cream,
  maraschino flavored or
  plain
Walnuts, chopped

Put 1 ladleful of finely chopped candied cherries in a large sundae dish and cover with 1 small ladleful of crushed pineapple. Put 3 small scoops of pistachio ice cream over the pineapple, spreading them out with a spoon. Top with whipped cream and a sprinkling of chopped walnuts.

Chocolate Banana Sundae

Banana, split in half
  lengthwise
Chocolate ice cream
Chocolate Walnut Sauce
  (recipe, see page 29)

Chocolate syrup
Chocolate Marshmallow
  Sauce (recipe, see
  page 27)
Chocolate shot

Place the split banana, cut sides up, in a banana split dish. Top with 2 scoops of chocolate ice cream. Over one, pour 1 ladle of Chocolate Walnut Sauce; over the other, 1 ladle of chocolate syrup. Top each with a dab of Chocolate Marshmallow Sauce and sprinkle with chocolate shot.

Chocolate Temptation Sundae

Chocolate ice cream
Chocolate Sauce (recipe, see
  page 31)

Roasted almonds, chopped
Whipped cream
Roasted almond, whole

Put 1 scoop of chocolate ice cream in a large sundae dish and top with Chocolate Sauce. Sprinkle with roasted almonds, cover with whipped cream, and top with a whole almond.

Clover Honey Sundae

Vanilla ice cream
Orange ice cream
Apricot Syrup (recipe, see
  page 27)

Walnuts, chopped
Whipped cream
Honey

Put 1 scoop each of vanilla and orange ice cream side by side in a sundae dish. Top each scoop with 1 generous tablespoon of Apricot Syrup mixed with walnuts. Cover with a circle of whipped cream forced through a pastry tube, and surround the base with a ribbon of whipped cream. Make small holes in the ribbon of whipped cream and fill them with honey.

*I*t takes approximately six months to train one **(soda jerk) properly.**

This famous and truly American creation is said to have originated at a time when the State of Massachusetts passed and enforced stringent laws prohibiting the sale of soft beverages of all kinds on Sundays. . . .

Creamallow Sundae

Chocolate ice cream　　*Walnut halves*
Marshmallow halves　　*Chocolate syrup*
Whipped cream

Place I scoop of chocolate ice cream in a sundae dish and surround it with 6 marshmallow halves. Cover the whole with whipped cream forced through a pastry tube and decorate with 6 walnut halves dipped in chocolate syrup.

Fan Tan Sundae

Strawberry ice cream　　*Whipped cream*
Figs, chopped　　*Pistachios, finely chopped*

Fill a glass two-thirds full of strawberry ice cream. Cover the ice cream with I ladle of chopped figs and top off the entire surface with whipped cream forced through a pastry bag. Dust with pistachios.

Half and Half Sundae

Vanilla ice cream	Pineapple, crushed
Ice, crushed	Whipped cream
Peaches, sliced	Cherry

Place I scoop of vanilla ice cream and I scoop of crushed ice side by side on a sundae plate. Pour I ladleful of sliced peaches over the ice cream and I ladleful of crushed pineapple over the ice. Smother the whole with whipped cream forced through a pastry tube and top with a cherry.

Knickerbocker Glory Sundae

Red currants, crushed	Kirsch
Peaches, crushed	Strawberry ice cream
Maraschino cherry juice	Whipped cream
Strawberries, crushed	Pistachios, chopped

Soak the currants and peaches separately in a little maraschino cherry juice and the strawberries in a little kirsch for I hour. Put I scoop of strawberry ice cream onto an oblong silver sundae dish and cover the ice cream with 2 tablespoons of strawberries and I teaspoon each of currants and peaches. Cover the entire surface crisscross fashion with whipped cream forced through a pastry tube. Sprinkle with chopped pistachios.

An enterprising confectioner merely omitted the carbonated water from the ice-cream soda, thus literally complying with the law. The name "Sundae" was applied to this product, and it has made a pleasing and palatable dish on weekdays as well as Sundays.

Sundaes should be served daintily, since nothing helps more to increase the volume of business, as well as the demand for sundaes, than dainty service. Daintiness goes beyond the dishes to actual service. Don't fill the sundaes so full that the dressing runs over the edge.

Maple Pecan Sundae

Vanilla ice cream
Maple syrup
Pecans, chopped

Ground cinnamon
Whipped cream

Put 1 scoop of vanilla ice cream into a dish, pour 1 ladle of maple syrup over it, and cover with chopped pecans. Sprinkle with a little ground cinnamon and top off with whipped cream.

Peach Royal Sundae

Whipped cream
Peaches, sliced
Vanilla ice cream

Pineapple, crushed
Walnuts, chopped
Cherry

Spread a sundae dish with whipped cream and arrange 6 slices of peaches over the whipped cream. In the center of the fruit, place 1 scoop of vanilla ice cream covered by 1 ladleful of crushed pineapple. Surround the base with a ribbon of whipped cream, sprinkle with walnuts, and top with a cherry.

FRESH FRUIT SUNDAE

FRESH PEACH SUNDAE

Ice-Cream Preparations

A soda dispenser with any degree of originality can invent sundaes almost as fast as he can think.

Siamese Twins Sundae

*Banana, split in half
  lengthwise
Chocolate ice cream*

*Chop Suey Sauce (recipe,
  see page 29)
Chocolate Marshmallow
  Sauce (recipe, see
  page 27)*

Place a split banana lengthwise on an oblong dish, cut sides up. Put 2 scoops of chocolate ice cream on it. Over each scoop pour a little Chop Suey Sauce and a little Chocolate Marshmallow Sauce.

Vanilla Mint Sundae

*Vanilla ice cream
Crème de menthe*

*Whipped cream
Fresh mint*

Over I scoop of ice cream pour I soda spoon of crème de menthe. Top with a tuft of whipped cream forced through a pastry tube. Garnish with a fresh mint leaf.

Strawberry Delight Sundae

Strawberry ice cream   Whipped cream
Strawberries, crushed   Strawberries, whole

Top I scoop of strawberry ice cream with I ladle of crushed strawberries. Around the base of the ice cream, make a double circle of whipped cream forced through a pastry tube. Drop a few whole strawberries into the whipped cream.

Skyscraper Sundae

Vanilla ice cream   Strawberry ice cream
Cherries, crushed   Whipped cream
Vanilla wafer   Cherry

Put 2 scoops of vanilla ice cream side by side on a large sundae dish and top with crushed cherries. Place I large vanilla wafer from scoop to scoop to form a bridge. In the center of the wafer, place a scoop of strawberry ice cream. Top with whipped cream and a cherry.

Capable soda jerks can make up any combination of ice cream and sherbets or frozen puddings; cover them with marshmallow, whipped cream, nuts, cherries, fresh or crystalized fruits, to make them look artistic, tempting, delicious; and give them a name.

Luncheonette

PARFAITS

A parfait is a sundae made with ice cream that is softer and creamier, served in a tall fluted glass called a parfait glass. In re-creating these parfaits, keep in mind that "the two requisites necessary to the serving of a good sundae (parfait) are pure, high-grade syrups and crushed fruits and a good grade of ice cream" (*Spatula Soda Water Guide*, 1905).

Broadway Parfait

Maple ice cream
Coffee ice cream
Whipped cream
Seedless raisins, chopped

Walnuts, chopped
Butterscotch syrup
Almonds, blanched
Chocolate syrup

Put 1 scoop of each maple and coffee ice cream into a glass. Add 1 ladle of whipped cream, 1 soda spoon of raisins, 1 spoon of chopped walnuts, and mix thoroughly with a spoon. Coat the inside of a parfait glass with butterscotch syrup and transfer the ice-cream mixture to the glass. Top with more whipped cream and a blanched almond dipped in chocolate syrup.

P arfait, which means "perfect" in French, differs from ice cream in that it is less cold and more creamy. This makes this dainty creation more delicate.

Whipped cream is usually served with both chocolate and cocoa. Instead, a marshmallow may be put into each serving before the beverage is poured in. This garnish is particularly favored by ladies.

Cafe Caramel Parfait

Butterscotch syrup
Coffee ice cream

Whipped cream

Spread the inner side of a parfait glass with a coating of butterscotch syrup. Put I scoop of coffee ice cream and I generous ladle of whipped cream into a glass, combining them rapidly to prevent ice cream from melting. When thoroughly mixed, transfer to the parfait glass, top with a ring of whipped cream, and fill the center with a little butterscotch syrup.

Crème de Menthe Parfait

Vanilla ice cream
Whipped cream

Crème de menthe
Cherries, crushed

Put I scoop of vanilla ice cream into a glass. Add I ladle of whipped cream, I soda spoon of crème de menthe, and 2 soda spoons of crushed cherries. Mix thoroughly with a spoon and transfer to a parfait glass. Top with more whipped cream.

Hollywood Parfait

Chocolate ice cream
Candied fruit, chopped
Vanilla Syrup (recipe, see
   page 27)

Marshmallow, quartered
Coffee ice cream
Whipped cream
Walnuts, finely chopped

Place I small scoop of chocolate ice cream into a parfait glass and sprinkle with I scant soda spoon of candied fruit. Mix lightly with a spoon. Pour on a little vanilla syrup and top with the quartered marshmallow and I small scoop of coffee ice cream. Cover with a generous portion of whipped cream forced through a pastry tube. Sprinkle with finely chopped walnuts.

Raspberry Parfait

Raspberry ice cream
Whipped cream

Raspberries

Put I scoop of raspberry ice cream and I generous ladle of whipped cream into a glass. Combine thoroughly with a spoon and transfer to a parfait glass. Top with whipped cream and a fresh raspberry or a bit of crushed raspberry.

When properly prepared and daintily served in an appropriate short-stemmed, tall, flute-shaped glass, called a parfait glass, the parfait is very tempting.

Certain parfaits may be decorated, but soberly. After topping the parfait with whipped cream forced through a pastry bag with a small fancy tip, top with a red or green maraschino cherry — cut daisy fashion or whole — an almond, nut half, pieces of candied fruit, or a fresh strawberry, raspberry, or a few red or white currants.

Maple Pecan Parfait

Maple ice cream
Whipped cream

Pecans, chopped
Pecan halves

Put 1 scoop of maple ice cream, 1 large ladle of whipped cream, and 2 soda spoons of chopped pecans into a glass. Mix thoroughly with a spoon and transfer to a parfait glass. Top with more whipped cream decorated with a pecan half.

Imperial Parfait

Vanilla ice cream
Almonds, chopped
Cherries, chopped
Strawberry ice cream

Chocolate syrup
Whipped cream
Pecan halves

Pack the bottom of a parfait glass one-third full with vanilla ice cream. Sprinkle a soda spoon of chopped almonds and one of chopped cherries over the ice cream. Top with a small scoop of strawberry ice cream. Let stand for a few minutes to allow the ice cream to soften slightly. Cover with chocolate syrup and whipped cream and decorate the top with a pecan half dipped in chocolate syrup.

*I*mportant: A glass of plain carbonated water or ice water is always served with a parfait.

The color and flavor of dressings should always contrast, yet harmonize with each other.

SYRUPS and SAUCES

DeGouy reminds us that "the difference that dressings make to an ice cream is . . . unbelievable." Though it is possible to purchase a large number of ice-cream sauces in your local supermarket, it is more fun and yields better results to make them at home. Use fresh fruits in season to produce sauces of wonderful taste and appearance.

Although syrups and sauces may be used interchangeably as toppings for sundaes and parfaits, sauces tend to be thicker and have more texture than syrups. In addition to providing an ice-cream topping, syrups also serve as flavorings in sodas, malts, and shakes.

Simple or Sugar Syrup

YIELDS 1 PINT

1³/₈ cup sugar   1¹/₄ cup hot water

Boil the sugar and hot water until the sugar is dissolved. This simple syrup may be flavored according to taste, using any of the dozens of flavoring extracts known on the market.

Flavored Syrups

Add ½ tablespoon of any of the extracts listed to 1 pint of Simple Syrup to obtain a flavored syrup. Increase the amount if a stronger flavor is desired.

The following extracts are available at supermarkets and gourmet shops: apricot, banana, lemon, lime, orange, peach, pineapple, raspberry, strawberry, vanilla.

For Coca-Cola syrup, add 5 or 6 tablespoons of Coca-Cola to 1 pint of Simple Syrup. Chocolate syrup, butterscotch syrup, and coffee syrup are readily available at supermarkets.

Chocolate Marshmallow Sauce

YIELDS 1 CUP

½ cup chocolate syrup *½ cup marshmallow fluff*

Combine the chocolate syrup and marshmallow fluff. Mix thoroughly.

For more sauce, raise the amount of ingredients; for less do the opposite.

Luncheonette

Chocolate Walnut Sauce

YIELDS 1½ CUPS

½ cup chocolate syrup   ½ cup walnuts, chopped
½ cup marshmallow fluff

Combine the chocolate syrup and marshmallow fluff thoroughly. Mix in the walnuts.

Chop Suey Sauce

YIELDS 1 CUP

¾ tablespoon chopped figs
¾ tablespoon chopped
   raisins
¾ tablespoon chopped
   dates
1½ tablespoons chopped
   walnuts

¾ tablespoon shredded
   coconut
⅔ tablespoon crushed
   cherries
⅔ tablespoon crushed
   pineapple
4 tablespoons maple syrup
4 tablespoons Simple Syrup
   (recipe, see page 26)

Combine all of the ingredients and keep in a crock jar. Stir well before using.

Serving an ice-cream dressing that is bland with a bland ice cream is not interesting.

The difference that dressings make to an ice cream is simply unbelievable. Dressing, garnishing, and trimming are to the decorative ensemble of a dish of ice cream, especially a sundae, what accessories are to a dress ensemble. And, like dress accessories, they should be chosen with taste, with a sure sense of their appropriateness.

Caramel Cream Sauce

YIELDS 2 CUPS

1 pound dark brown sugar   ¼ cup butter
                              1 cup heavy cream

Combine the sugar, butter, and cream in a double boiler. Let cook, stirring occasionally until thick. Cool and keep covered in the refrigerator until needed. To use, place the jar in hot water. Reheating enriches the flavor.

Raisin Cream Sauce

YIELDS 1 CUP

⅔ cup seedless raisins,   ½ cup heavy cream
    chopped   ½ cup powdered sugar

Combine the raisins, cream, and powdered sugar. Boil until thick enough to be of running consistency. Keep in a cool place.

Variation: Hazelnut Cream Sauce. Substitute roasted chopped hazelnuts for the raisins.

Chocolate Sauce

YIELDS 1 CUP

2 squares unsweetened
chocolate
¼ cup water
½ cup granulated sugar

Salt
5 tablespoons butter
¼ teaspoon vanilla extract

Add the chocolate to the water and cook over a low flame, stirring until blended and smooth. Add the sugar and a pinch of salt and continue cooking, stirring constantly until the sugar is dissolved and the mixture slightly thickened. Add the butter and vanilla extract and immediately remove from heat. This keeps well when cooled and placed in the refrigerator. Reheat over hot water.

Variation: Chocolate Mint Sauce. Substitute ½ teaspoon of peppermint extract for the vanilla extract.

Marshmallow Cream Sauce

YIELDS 1 CUP

⅔ cup marshmallow fluff   ⅓ cup heavy cream

Blend the marshmallow fluff and heavy cream. If a richer mixture is desired, use more cream. The mixture should be the consistency of heavy cream. Do not prepare too much in advance since this does not keep well.

These dressings can be prepared from various fruits, nuts, and syrups and are used in practically the same manner as the ordinary crushed fruits. They are easily prepared and should always be on hand.

ICE-CREAM SODAS

Robert Green of Philadelphia was selling a concoction of syrup, sweet cream, and soda water at the semicentennial celebration of the Franklin Institute in Philadelphia in 1874 when he ran out of cream and substituted vanilla ice cream, thus creating a new beverage, the ice-cream soda. In fact, the term "soda fountain" originally connoted an apparatus for producing carbonated water that was capable of regulating the stream of water to create a variety of effects. When making these sodas (or your own creations), use a soda water siphon to create the same effect. Alternately, you may use bottled club soda or seltzer.

Banana Soda

Banana Syrup (recipe, see
  page 27)
Soda water

Vanilla ice cream
Whipped cream

Draw 4 tablespoons of Banana Syrup into a glass. Carbonate two-thirds full with soda water, add 1 scoop of vanilla ice cream, and finish with more soda water. Top off with whipped cream.

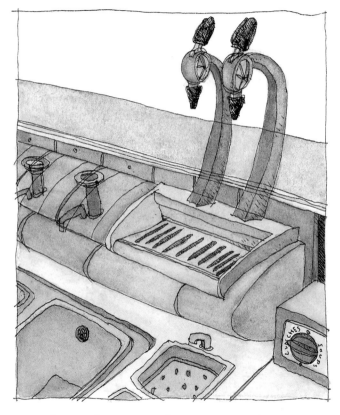

Special attention should be given to the carbonator at all times. This machine, once installed, will not go on and do its work efficiently unless it receives the proper care.

There are fancy ice-cream sodas called ice-cream floats. These are made by floating a small dipper of ice cream on a glass of soda previously drawn and mixed as an ordinary ice-cream soda. The soda is drawn as plain soda, solid without foam. . . .

Coffee Soda

Coffee syrup
Soda water

Chocolate ice cream
Whipped cream

Draw 4 tablespoons of coffee syrup into a glass. Carbonate with a fine stream of soda water until two-thirds full, add 1 scoop of chocolate ice cream, and finish with a fine stream of soda water. Top with whipped cream.

Maple Soda

Maple syrup (use the best
   Vermont maple syrup you
   can find)
Soda water

Vanilla ice cream
Chocolate ice cream
Whipped cream
Chocolate shot

Dispense 4 tablespoons of maple syrup into a glass. Carbonate with a fine stream of soda until two-thirds full. Add ½ scoop each of vanilla and chocolate ice cream. Finish with a fine stream of soda and top off with 1 soda spoon of whipped cream sprinkled with chocolate shot.

Gloucester Soda

Grenadine syrup (available
   at gourmet shops,
   supermarkets, and liquor
   stores)

Soda water
Maple walnut ice cream
Whipped cream

Draw 4 tablespoons of grenadine into a glass and carbonate with soda until two-thirds full. Add 1 scoop of maple walnut ice cream, finish with soda water, and top off with whipped cream.

Chocolate Soda

Chocolate syrup
Soda water

Chocolate ice cream
Whipped cream

Dispense 4 tablespoons of chocolate syrup into a glass. Carbonate with a fine stream of soda water until two-thirds full. Add 1 scoop of chocolate ice cream, and finish with a fine stream of soda. Top off with 1 soda spoon of whipped cream. Serve with straws.

The glass is not quite filled, leaving room enough for the portion of ice cream desired. Sometimes the ice cream is topped with crushed fruit. Every ice-cream soda may be transformed into an ice-cream float. The small scoop of ice cream must be neatly shaped.

Luncheonette

Minnehaha Soda

Vanilla Syrup (recipe, see
  page 27)
Soda water
Strawberry ice cream

Raspberry ice cream
Whipped cream
Grated orange rind

Draw 4 tablespoons of Vanilla Syrup into a glass. Carbonate with a fine stream of soda until two-thirds full. Add ½ scoop each of strawberry and raspberry ice cream. Finish with a fine stream of soda. Top off with I soda spoon of whipped cream and sprinkle with a little grated orange rind.

Peter Pan Soda

Peach Syrup (recipe, see
  page 27)
Soda water

Vanilla ice cream
Whipped cream

Draw 4 tablespoons of Peach Syrup into a glass and carbonate with a fine stream of soda until two-thirds full. Add I scoop of vanilla ice cream. Finish with a fine stream of soda and top off with I soda spoon of whipped cream.

When you are whipping heavy cream, care should be taken that the bowl and beater are chilled as well as the cream, for the high temperature of the air can very quickly warm the cream to a point where it will not whip successfully.

Cream must be cold to whip well. Aging improves the whipping qualities of cream also.

Pineapple Soda

Pineapple Syrup (recipe, see page 27)
Soda water

Pineapple ice cream
Whipped cream

Draw 4 tablespoons of Pineapple Syrup into a glass. Carbonate with soda until two-thirds full. Add I scoop of pineapple ice cream, finish with soda, and top with whipped cream.

Strawberry Soda

Strawberry Syrup (recipe, see page 27)
Soda water

Strawberry ice cream
Whipped cream

Dispense 4 tablespoons of Strawberry Syrup into a glass. Carbonate with a fine stream of soda until two-thirds full. Add I scoop of strawberry ice cream, finish with a fine stream of soda, and top off with I soda spoon of whipped cream.

Susie Soda

Simple Syrup (recipe, see
  page 26)
Soda water

Raspberry ice cream
Whipped cream
Strawberries, crushed

Draw 4 tablespoons of Simple Syrup into a glass. Carbonate two-thirds full of soda, add 1 scoop of raspberry ice cream, and finish with a fine stream of soda. Top the whole with whipped cream and 1 soda spoon of crushed strawberries.

Vanilla Soda

Vanilla Syrup (recipe, see
  page 27)
Soda water

Strawberry ice cream
Whipped cream

Draw 4 tablespoons of Vanilla Syrup into a glass. Carbonate two-thirds full of soda, add 1 scoop of strawberry ice cream, and top off with soda water. Garnish with whipped cream.

Cream that has stood one or two days whips better than cream that is just a few hours old, providing of course that it has been kept cold.

BEVERAGES

FLIPS

DeGouy describes the flip as "a rich drink which may be made with almost any type of syrup. It should be made very rapidly and always shaken when served cold, never stirred. A whole egg or an egg yolk, slightly spiced and sugared, and syrup or fruit juice . . . are usually used. The mixture is strained into a 10-ounce glass and diluted with carbonated water if cold, and hot water if hot." In the 1930s and 40s' a bit of phosphate would be added to the flip to create foam. The addition of an egg and vigorous shaking or whirring in a blender produces the same result.

Coffee Flip

Coffee syrup
Vanilla Syrup (recipe, see
  page 27)
Whole egg

Nutmeg or cinnamon
Ice, crushed
Soda water
Whipped cream

Draw 3 tablespoons of coffee syrup and 1 scant tablespoon of Vanilla Syrup into a shaker. Break a fresh egg into the shaker and add a few grains of nutmeg or cinnamon and a little crushed ice. Shake vigorously, fill with soda water, and strain into a glass. Top off with whipped cream.

Perhaps the American beverage with the longest history is the flip. This beverage was popular with Paul Revere and most of the folks of the time. The flip was the mainstay of the tavern and the tavern was the town hall and clubhouse of the time.

*T*o be sure an egg is strictly fresh, break it into a clean glass before dropping it into the shaker.

Hot Lemon Flip

Lemon Syrup (recipe, see
  page 27)
Lime Syrup (recipe, see
  page 27)

Whole egg
Ice, crushed
Hot water
Lemon peel

Draw 2 tablespoons of Lemon Syrup and 1 tablespoon of Lime Syrup into a shaker. Break a fresh egg into the shaker, add a little crushed ice, and shake vigorously. Fill with hot water and strain into a glass. Top off with a twist of lemon peel.

Miami Flip

Raspberry Syrup (recipe, see
  page 27)
Orange Syrup (recipe, see
  page 27)
Whole egg

Lime juice, fresh
Ice, crushed
Soda water
Orange slice
Cherry

Dispense 2 tablespoons of Raspberry Syrup and 1 tablespoon of Orange Syrup into a shaker. Into this break a fresh egg, add 4 or 5 dashes of fresh lime juice and a little crushed ice, and shake vigorously. Fill with soda and strain into a glass. Top off with a thin slice of orange and a cherry stuck with a toothpick.

Royal Flip

Vanilla Syrup (recipe, see
  page 27)
Pineapple Syrup (recipe, see
  page 27)
Raspberry Syrup (recipe, see
  page 27)

Whole egg
Ice, crushed
Vanilla ice cream
Soda water
Cherry

Draw 1 tablespoon each of Vanilla, Pineapple, and Raspberry syrups into a shaker. Add a fresh egg, some crushed ice, and shake vigorously. Add 1 small scoop of vanilla ice cream and shake again. Fill with soda, strain into a glass, and top off with a cherry.

Strawberry Flip

Strawberry Syrup (recipe,
  see page 27)
Lemon Syrup (recipe, see
  page 27)

Whole egg
Ice, crushed
Soda water
Whipped cream

Into a shaker, put 3 tablespoons of Strawberry Syrup, 1 tablespoon of Lemon Syrup, a fresh egg, and some crushed ice. Shake vigorously, fill with soda, and strain into a glass. Top with a tuft of whipped cream.

A flip should always be "flipped," that is, shaken rapidly, lightly, and pertly, thus obtaining a foamy beverage that when cold should be really cold and when hot should be really hot. Hot or cold, flips may be garnished with fresh fruits in season.

FIZZES

Fizzes are refreshing light beverages consisting quite simply of syrup, soda, powdered sugar to create the fizz, and occasionally an egg white for foam. As DeGouy reminds us, they should "always be served fizzing."

Golden Fizz

Lemon Syrup (recipe, see
  page 27)
Egg yolk

Ground ginger
Soda water
Powdered sugar

Draw 3 tablespoons of Lemon Syrup into a glass. Add an egg yolk, 3 dashes of ginger, and fill with soda to within 1 inch of the top. Stir in ½ soda spoon of powdered sugar. Serve while fizzing.

Orange Fizz

Orange Syrup (recipe, see
  page 27)
Lemon Syrup (recipe, see
  page 27)

Orange
Soda water
Powdered sugar

Draw 3 tablespoons of Orange Syrup, 1 tablespoon of Lemon Syrup, and the juice of ½ orange into a glass. Fill with soda water to within 1 inch of the top. Stir in ½ soda spoon of powdered sugar. Serve while fizzing.

*T*oday the importance of fruit juices is well recognized, hence such great demand, especially by ladies. Some of the most popular fruit juices are orange, pineapple, grapefruit, cranberry, grape, and apple juice.

izzes are usually served in a 10-ounce glass and should always be served while fizzing.

Pittsburgh Fizz

Orange Syrup (recipe, see
   page 27)
Orange juice
Lemon juice
Orange flower water
   (available at gourmet
   shops)

Egg white
Ice, crushed
Soda water
Powdered sugar

Put 3 tablespoons of Orange Syrup, the juice of 1 orange, the juice of ½ lemon, and 5 dashes of orange flower water into a shaker. Drop in a fresh egg white, add a little crushed ice, and shake vigorously. Strain into a glass and fill with soda to within 1 inch of the top. Stir in 1 soda spoon of powdered sugar. Serve while fizzing.

EGGNOGS

*T*he soda fountain beverages based on milk, cream, or buttermilk are much richer than those based on soda. Perhaps the richest of these is the eggnog, which consists of a fresh egg, cream, milk, or ice cream, and syrup. This mixture is shaken vigorously, strained, and served immediately. The *Spatula Soda Water Guide* of 1905 states that "no other drink requires the skill and study in order that it may be properly made as the egg drink does. Perfection in mixing them is not reached in a month, nor in a year either. It takes years of practice to become perfect."

Chocolate Eggnog

Chocolate syrup
Whole egg
Ice, crushed

Milk
Nutmeg

Draw 3 tablespoons of chocolate syrup into a shaker. Break a fresh egg into the shaker and add a little crushed ice. Fill up to two thirds with cold milk, shake vigorously, and strain into a glass. Top off with grated nutmeg.

Christmas Eggnog

Pineapple Syrup (recipe, see page 27)
Orange Syrup (recipe, see page 27)
Vanilla Syrup (recipe, see page 27)

Whole egg
Orange flower water (available at gourmet shops)
Vanilla ice cream
Milk

Draw 1 tablespoon each of Pineapple, Orange, and Vanilla syrups into a shaker. Add a fresh egg, a dash of orange flower water, and 1 small scoop of vanilla ice cream. Fill the shaker two-thirds full of milk, shake vigorously, and strain into a glass.

Use fresh fruit in season to give color and class to the glass; a slice of orange, lemon, lime; a cluster of cherries or fresh berries whole or halved to float on the top.

*g*t really seems as if it would be simple to make good coffee, but a good cup of coffee depends upon so many things besides the actual making, although that is important. Good coffee is clean and sparkling and of fine flavor.

Luncheonette

Coffee Eggnog

Coffee syrup
Vanilla Syrup (recipe, see
  page 27)

Heavy cream
Whole egg
Ice, crushed

Put 3 tablespoons of coffee syrup, 1 tablespoon of Vanilla Syrup, and 2 tablespoons of heavy cream into a shaker. Break a fresh egg into the shaker, add a little ice, and shake vigorously. Strain into a glass.

Malted Chocolate Eggnog

Chocolate syrup
Whole egg
Malted milk powder

Ice, crushed
Milk

Put three tablespoons of chocolate syrup, a fresh egg, and 2 soda spoons of malted milk powder into a shaker. Add a little crushed ice, fill with cold milk, and shake vigorously. Strain into a glass.

Eggnogs are usually served with wafers or crackers.

Hot days call for innocuous drinks, but make them look dangerous, make them look smart.

New Orleans Eggnog

Molasses
Heavy cream
Whole egg
Nutmeg

Vanilla ice cream
Ice, crushed
Milk

Put 3 tablespoons of molasses and 1 tablespoon of heavy cream into a shaker. Break a fresh egg and let it drop into the shaker. Add a dash of grated nutmeg, 1 small scoop of vanilla ice cream, a little crushed ice, and fill with cold milk. Shake vigorously and strain into a glass.

Orange Eggnog

Orange Syrup (recipe, see page 27)
Whole egg

Heavy cream
Milk

Draw 3 tablespoons of Orange Syrup into a shaker. Add a fresh egg and 2 tablespoons of cream. Fill the glass with cold milk, shake vigorously, and strain into a glass.

Strawberry Eggnog

Strawberry Syrup (recipe,
  see page 27)
Raspberry Syrup (recipe, see
  page 27)
Heavy cream

Whole egg
Milk
Whipped cream
Nutmeg

Draw 2 tablespoons of Strawberry Syrup, 1 tablespoon of Raspberry Syrup, and 4 tablespoons of cream into a shaker. Break a fresh egg into the shaker, fill with cold milk, and shake vigorously. Strain into a glass, top off with whipped cream, and dust with nutmeg.

MALTED MILK SHAKES

*M*alted milk shakes are prepared in the same manner as eggnogs, but they usually call for malted milk powder instead of the egg. Malted milk powder is made from dehydrated whole milk and malted barley and wheat extracts, and is available at most supermarkets. If an egg is added, the shake becomes a malted nog. While most malted milk shakes are served cold, there were some that were served hot. We have provided a recipe for a hot malted milk to warm you in cold weather. Malted milk shakes may be prepared in a blender.

Fruit drinks without spirits demand sophistication. Pay strict attention to their detail. Serve them with straws and a crisp topknot of mint.

When preparing a malted beverage, never add ice into it. The liquid ingredients composing the beverage should be ice cold, except when egg is added to the beverage. A malted beverage should be shaken well and rapidly.

Chocolate Malted Milk

Chocolate syrup
Malted milk powder
Chocolate ice cream

Milk
Whipped cream

Draw 3 tablespoons of chocolate syrup into a shaker. Add 3 soda spoons of malted milk powder, I scoop of chocolate ice cream, and milk. Mix well. Top off with whipped cream.

Coca-Cola Malted Milk

Coca-Cola Syrup (recipe, see page 27)
Chocolate syrup
Heavy cream

Malted milk powder
Soda water
Whipped cream or chocolate ice cream

Into a shaker, put I tablespoon each of Coca-Cola and chocolate syrup, 4 tablespoons of heavy cream, and 2 soda spoons of malted milk powder. Shake vigorously, strain into a glass, and fill with soda water. Top off with either whipped cream or chocolate ice cream.

Beverages

*C*old malted milk beverages should always be served in a 12-ounce glass and hot ones in a mug. The cold ones may be topped with whipped cream, and the hot ones with nutmeg.

Hot Malted Milk

Chocolate, coffee, or Vanilla
  Syrup (recipe, see page 27)
Malted milk powder
Salt

Milk, hot
Cinnamon, nutmeg, or
  whipped cream

Draw 2 tablespoons of desired syrup into a mixing glass. Add 3 soda spoons of malted milk powder, a few grains of salt, 4 tablespoons of hot milk, and blend well. Stir in enough milk to fill the mug. Dust the top with cinnamon, nutmeg, or whipped cream, as desired.

    Chocolate, coffee, or vanilla flavoring may be used, according to call. This drink should be served in a heated mug.

Imperial Malted Milk

Pineapple Syrup (recipe, see
  page 27)
Malted milk powder
Vanilla ice cream

Milk
Whipped cream
Nutmeg

Draw 3 tablespoons of Pineapple Syrup into a blender. Add 1 tablespoon of malted milk powder, 1 scoop of vanilla ice cream, and cold milk. Blend thoroughly. Pour into a glass and top with whipped cream and grated nutmeg.

MILK SHAKES

*T*he simplest of the milk-based soda fountain beverages is the milk shake, which is made with syrup, milk or buttermilk, and sometimes ice cream. These simple ingredients can be mixed in a variety of ways to create thoroughly satisfying beverages that range from the familiar coffee to the unusual tomato shake. Milk shakes may be made in a blender.

Malted Milk Egg Shake

Chocolate, coffee, or Vanilla
* Syrup (recipe, see page 27)*
Malted milk powder
Whole egg

Ice, crushed
Milk
Nutmeg or cinnamon

Into a shaker draw 2 tablespoons of desired syrup. Add I tablespoon of malted milk powder, a fresh egg, and a little crushed ice. Fill with cold milk and shake. Strain into a glass and top off with a little nutmeg or cinnamon.

ce there must be in glacier supply.

***m**ilk shakes are usu-ally served in 12-ounce glasses, as are buttermilk shakes. Cream shakes are served in 10-ounce glasses. All are served with straws, hot or cold.*

Luncheonette

Brown Cow Shake

Chocolate syrup
Evaporated milk
Root beer

Ice, crushed
Chocolate shot

Draw 2 tablespoons of chocolate syrup into a shaker, add enough evaporated milk to fill the shaker half full, and fill up to two thirds with root beer. Add a little crushed ice and shake vigorously. Strain into a glass and dust with chocolate shot. Serve with straws.

Buttermilk Chocolate Shake

Chocolate syrup
Buttermilk

Ice, crushed
Soda water

Into a shaker draw 2 tablespoons of chocolate syrup. Fill three-quarters full of buttermilk, add a little crushed ice, and shake vigorously. Strain into a glass and fill with a fine stream of soda just to liven it a little.

Cold drinks depend for their appeal almost as much on sight and sound as they do on flavor.

Buttermilk Vanilla Shake

Vanilla ice cream   *Buttermilk*

Put I scoop of vanilla ice cream into a shaker. Fill the glass with buttermilk, shake vigorously, and strain into a glass. Serve with a straw.

Coffee Milk Shake

Coffee syrup   *Milk*

Draw 4 tablespoons of coffee syrup into a shaker. Fill with milk, shake vigorously, and strain into a glass. Serve with a straw.

Hot Milk Shake

Hot milk shakes are made exactly as cold milk shakes, except that hot milk is substituted for cold. Almost any kind of flavor may be used. Serve as hot as possible. Serve with straws.

Chocolate Peanut Shake

Chocolate syrup   Milk
Peanut butter   Vanilla ice cream

Put 3 tablespoons of chocolate syrup and 1 tablespoon of peanut butter into a shaker. Fill with cold milk, shake vigorously, and top with a scoop of vanilla ice cream. Serve with a spoon.

Chocolate Custard Shake

Chocolate syrup   Whole egg, separated
Pineapple Syrup (recipe, see   Vanilla ice cream
  page 27)   Soda water

Draw 2 tablespoons of chocolate syrup into one glass and 2 tablespoons of Pineapple Syrup into another. Add the egg white to the chocolate syrup and the yolk to the Pineapple Syrup. Beat both thoroughly, then mix together. Add 1 scoop of vanilla ice cream and beat the whole thoroughly with an electric mixer. Top off glass with soda. Serve with a spoon.

The plainest drink may be made impressive. In order to obtain the full refreshing flavor of the cooling beverage, especially those in which fruit and fruit juices are used, serve them as soon as dispensed.

Almost any kind of syrup or ice cream may be used in the preparation of these popular beverages.

Luncheonette

Cream of Cocoa Shake

Chocolate syrup
Ice, crushed
Heavy cream

Milk
Whipped cream
Chocolate shot

Draw 3 tablespoons of chocolate syrup into a shaker. Fill one-third full of crushed ice. Add 4 tablespoons of cream, fill with cold milk, shake vigorously, and strain into a glass. Top with whipped cream and sprinkle with chocolate shot.

Creole Milk Shake

Chocolate syrup
Soda water
Egg yolk

Ice, crushed
Milk
Cinnamon

Into a shaker draw 3 tablespoons of chocolate syrup. Add 3 dashes of soda, the fresh egg yolk, and a little crushed ice. Fill up to two-thirds full with cold milk. Shake vigorously, strain into a glass, and dust with cinnamon. Serve with straws.

milk shakes should be vigorously shaken with a little shaved ice and the glass filled two-thirds full to allow the foam to fill up the balance. They may be dusted with ground nutmeg or cinnamon, or sometimes with chocolate shot.

The soda fountain lunch should be easy to prepare, quickly done, and daintily served. Yet keep in mind your first objective is selling ice cream and beverages.

Philadelphia Orange Cream Shake

Orange Syrup (recipe, see
  page 27)
Egg yolk
Cream

Milk
Lemon rind, grated
Nutmeg

Draw 2 tablespoons of Orange Syrup into a shaker. Add an egg yolk and equal parts of cream and milk. Shake vigorously, strain into a glass, and garnish with grated lemon rind mixed with nutmeg. Serve with a straw.

Prune Juice Milk Shake

Lemon Syrup (recipe, see
  page 27)
Prune juice

Ice, crushed
Milk

Into a shaker put 1 tablespoon of Lemon Syrup and 6 tablespoons of prune juice. Add a little crushed ice, fill with cold milk, and shake. Strain into a glass. Serve with straws.

Tomato Milk Shake

Tomato puree   Nutmeg
Lemon juice   Lemon peel
Milk

Put 5 tablespoons of tomato puree and a few drops of lemon juice into a shaker. Fill with milk, shake, and strain into a glass. Dust with nutmeg and garnish with a twist of lemon peel.

Lemon Milk Shake

Lemon Syrup (recipe, see   Ice, crushed
  page 27)   Milk
Lemon   Lemon rind, grated

Draw 3 tablespoons of Lemon Syrup into a shaker. Add juice of ¼ lemon, some crushed ice, and fill up to two-thirds with cold milk. Shake vigorously. Strain into a 12-ounce glass, dust with a little lemon rind, and serve with straws.

Though people as a rule do not tire of tomato juice, you may wish to vary your manner of serving it.

SANDWICHES

SODA FOUNTAIN SAVORIES

Prior to Prohibition, bars and saloons often served free lunches along with alcoholic beverages. When these establishments were forced to close, many men joined women and children at the soda fountain, and fountain proprietors began adding some simple luncheon foods to their menus. The fountain came to be a place where working people could have an inexpensive, well-prepared lunch — accompanied, of course, by a soda or finished with a sundae.

This was a time when sandwiches were "built," not simply made, and all sandwiches were served with an attractive and appropriate garnish. Fanned pickles, chopped eggs, stuffed olives, pepper rings, paprika, and tomato slices were only a few of the garnishes used to dress up a sandwich plate.

Sandwich servings are for one unless otherwise indicated.

SINGLE SANDWICHES

Properly made, sandwiches contain well-balanced food combinations that are both delicious and wholesome. In preparing meat fillings, cut the meat approximately the same size as the bread. One and a half ounces of meat is enough for a tasty single sandwich.

The only way to make a sandwich successfully is with the hands. In trimming a sandwich, place the thumb flat in the center of the bread and the other fingers at the left corner. As the bread is trimmed, these fingers pull the sandwich around. Cut the sandwich diagonally from corner to corner and put it on a plate to give a diamond effect.

good sandwich must be built out to the corners or it makes a bad impression on the guest when it is picked up.

American Cheese and Peanut Butter Sandwich

Peanut or apple butter
White sandwich bread
American cheese

Watercress
Tomato slice
Green olive

Spread peanut or apple butter thinly on 1 slice of sandwich bread, cover with thin slices of American cheese, and top with bread. Cut the sandwich from corner to corner, making four triangles. Garnish the center of the sandwiches with a small bunch of crisp watercress. Decorate with a slice of tomato topped with an olive.

Hamburger Sandwich

Hamburger steak patties
White bread or roll
Mustard

Brown gravy
Buttered peas

Place 1 or 2 hamburger steak patties on top of 1 slice of bread, toast, or split roll spread with prepared mustard. Cover with brown gravy. Garnish according to taste and serve with 1 scoop of buttered peas.

Ham and Egg Sandwich

Ham slice   Whole wheat bread
Egg   Olive

Fry a slice of ham on one side. Turn it over and break an egg onto it. When the egg begins to harden, turn the ham and egg over and cook the egg on the other side, breaking the yolk. Serve between slices of whole wheat bread and garnish with an olive.

Cottage Cheese, Honey, and Nut Sandwich

Whole wheat bread, toasted   Honey
Butter   Lettuce
Cottage cheese   Tomato slice
Walnuts, chopped

Butter the toast and spread on a mixture of equal parts of cottage cheese, walnuts, and honey, thoroughly blended. Top with a leaf of lettuce and another slice of toast. Cut diagonally and garnish with a slice of tomato.

*O*nly cut sandwiches into four pieces on request. It slows up service and makes it harder to pick up a sandwich and put it on a plate.

Two kinds of bread make an interesting and tasty sandwich. It is best always to get good bread. If bread is not even, if the texture is not right, it will not toast evenly regardless of how good the toaster is. Very even toast is essential.

Roquefort Cheese and Worcestershire Sauce Sandwich

Roquefort cheese
Worcestershire sauce
White bread, toasted

Lettuce
Pineapple, shredded

Cream 2 tablespoons of Roquefort cheese with a generous dash of Worcestershire sauce. Spread over freshly made toast. Cover with toast and cut from corner to corner, making four triangular sandwiches. Serve garnished with a small lettuce cup filled with shredded pineapple.

Western Sandwich

Egg
Chicken, cooked, chopped
Pimiento, chopped
Butter
White bread, toasted
Horseradish blended with
  butter

Broiled tomato slice
Lettuce
Black olive
Cream cheese mixed with
  chopped walnuts

Beat an egg slightly and add 1 tablespoon each of chicken and pimiento. Fry the mixture in butter on both sides and serve on toast spread with horseradish butter. Garnish with a tomato slice placed upon a crisp lettuce leaf. Top with a large black olive stuffed with the cream cheese—walnut mixture.

Sandwiches

For interest and variety put your ingredients on different breads, such as cream cheese on nut bread or corned beef on pumpernickel. Your trade will appreciate it and your employees will take greater interest in developing and discovering new menu items.

CLUB or THREE-DECKER SANDWICHES

Club or three-decker sandwiches are made of three slices of bread that may be plain or toasted, and served hot or cold. They may be cut in halves diagonally or into thirds or quarters.

Apricot-Ham on Toast

White bread, toasted
Apricots, cooked, chopped
Lettuce

Ham
Mayonnaise

Lower layer: apricots covered with lettuce. Second layer: ham covered with lettuce and mayonnaise.

Bacon-Cucumber and Asparagus Tips on Rye

Rye bread
Bacon, broiled
Cucumber, sliced

Lettuce
Asparagus tips
French dressing

Lower layer: broiled bacon covered with cucumber slices and lettuce. Second layer: shredded lettuce tossed with French dressing and asparagus tips.

Bacon-Orange Marmalade and Banana on Rye

Rye bread
Bacon, broiled
Lettuce

Orange marmalade
Banana, sliced

Lower layer: bacon covered with lettuce. Second layer: orange marmalade topped with banana slices and a lettuce leaf.

Egg-Swiss Cheese and Ham-Tomato-Lettuce on Toasted Rye

Rye bread, toasted
Egg, hard-boiled, sliced
Swiss cheese, sliced
Mustard

Lettuce
Ham, sliced
Tomato, sliced

Lower layer: sliced egg, Swiss cheese, spread with mustard and topped with lettuce leaves. Second layer: thinly sliced ham, tomato, and lettuce leaves.

The lower layer (of a club sandwich) is filled with a spread or filling, topped with another slice of bread, filled with a spread or filling, topped with another slice of bread, gently pressed together with the tips of the fingers and the sandwich knife, and cut according to order or fancy. When cut into thirds or quarters, they may be held together with toothpicks.

L u n c h e o n e t t e

Hamburger-Egg and Orange Marmalade-Lettuce on Nut Bread

Nut bread
Hamburger, broiled
Egg, hard-boiled, sliced

Watercress
Orange marmalade
Lettuce, shredded

Lower layer: hamburger, sliced egg, watercress. Second layer: orange marmalade, shredded lettuce.

Peanut Butter-Sardine and Potato Salad-Lettuce on Rye

Rye bread
Peanut butter
Boneless sardines

Lettuce, shredded
Potato salad

Lower layer: peanut butter topped with a sardine and shredded lettuce. Second layer: potato salad topped with lettuce.

*G*arnishing dishes today is more imperative than ever before on account of keen competition.

A knife and fork should be served with thick or moist sandwiches.

Tuna Salad-Pimiento and Sliced Egg-Green Pepper Rings on Rye

Rye bread
Tuna Fish Spread (recipe,
 see page 87)
Pimiento, chopped
Watercress, chopped

Egg, hard-boiled, sliced
Horseradish
Green pepper rings
Lettuce

Lower layer: Tuna Fish Salad topped with pimiento and watercress. Second layer: egg slices spread with horseradish and topped with green pepper rings and lettuce leaves

SPREADS *and* FILLINGS

Canapés offer a fertile field for the originality of the chef and generous is the reward when tempting canapés are presented. As DeGouy reminds us, sandwich spreads and fillings may be used on canapés as well as in sandwiches. They may be served on toast cut into fancy shapes such as stars, circles, triangles, or fingers, and attractively garnished.

One cup of filling provides enough for seven sandwiches. Feel free to adjust the ingredients and seasonings to suit your own taste.

Anchovy Parmesan Cheese Spread

YIELDS 1 SERVING

5 tablespoons grated
Parmesan cheese

1 1/2 tablespoons anchovy
paste
Mayonnaise

Combine the freshly grated Parmesan with the anchovy paste. Moisten with a little mayonnaise.

Apple and Peanut Butter Spread

YIELDS 1 CUP

10 tablespoons finely
chopped apple
1 teaspoon lemon juice

4 tablespoons peanut
butter, softened
Mayonnaise

Combine the apple with the lemon juice. Mix with the softened peanut butter combined with a bit of mayonnaise.

The idea in making a sandwich is to build it so that when it is trimmed, there is no waste. It is much better to put an extra piece of meat on the sandwich and give the benefit to the guest than to leave it to wastage.

When making sand-wiches and ca-napés, use two or three kinds of bread; change from white to rye, to wheat, to raisin, to orange, to banana, to apricot. Change often.

Apricot Filling

YIELDS 1 CUP

²/₃ cup dried apricots
³/₈ cup granulated sugar
¹/₄ orange rind, shredded

¹/₄ cup seedless raisins
¹/₄ cup chopped walnuts

Soak the apricots in cold water for 4 hours. Drain and chop. Combine the apricots with the sugar, orange rind, raisins, and walnuts. Cook over a gentle fire for 1 hour, stirring occasionally. Cool and chill.

Cottage Cheese Filling

YIELDS 1½ CUPS

1 cup cottage cheese
2 tablespoons minced
   chives
2 tablespoons grated onion

2 tablespoons minced
   parsley
Salt
White pepper

Combine the cheese with the chives, onion, and parsley, and season with salt and pepper.

*A*ny kind of sandwich should be daintily, soberly garnished before being presented to patrons.

The difference that garnishings make to a dish, be it a plain or an elaborate one, is simply unbelievable until you see it with your own eyes. Garnishing, decorating, and trimming are to the decorative ensemble of a dish what accessories are to a dress ensemble.

Avocado Spread

YIELDS 1 CUP

2 medium-sized avocados,
    mashed
1 tablespoon lemon juice

1 tablespoon minced onion
Salt

Season the avocado with lemon juice, grated onion, and salt to taste.

Carrot Filling

YIELDS 1½ CUPS

1 cup grated raw carrots
5 tablespoons mayonnaise
1 teaspoon salt
    Pinch of pepper

½ cup chopped walnuts
1 tablespoon lemon juice
    Dash of Worcestershire
    sauce

Combine the carrots, mayonnaise, salt, pepper, walnuts, lemon juice, and Worcestershire sauce. Blend well.

Chicken Filling

YIELDS 1½ CUPS

½ cup chopped cooked
   chicken
3 green olives, chopped
2 eggs, hard-boiled,
   chopped

½ green pepper, chopped
1½ teaspoons chili sauce
3 tablespoons mayonnaise
   Worcestershire sauce

Blend the chicken, olives, eggs, and green pepper. Add the chili sauce, mayonnaise, and a few drops of Worcestershire sauce.

Baked Bean Spread

YIELDS 1 CUP

1 cup baked beans,
   mashed
1 teaspoon horseradish

2 teaspoons mustard
2 teaspoons catsup

Combine the baked beans with the horseradish, mustard, and catsup.

Like dress accessories, garnishes should be chosen with taste and a sure sense of their appropriateness. The shape, color, and edible texture of these accessories should always be suitable to the dish in which they are used, and should harmonize with the decorative scheme of the dish, exactly like the makeup of a woman.

Luncheonette

Chicken Liver Spread

YIELDS 1 CUP

1 cup mashed, cooked   2 ½ teaspoons mustard
   chicken livers   1 ½ teaspoons catsup
1 teaspoon horseradish

Season the mashed chicken livers with the horseradish, mustard, and catsup.

Crabmeat Spread

YIELDS 1 CUP

1 cup chopped crabmeat   2 tablespoons minced
2 tablespoons minced   onion
   celery   ½ teaspoon curry powder
          6 tablespoons mayonnaise

Combine the crabmeat with the celery and onion. Blend the curry powder to taste with the mayonnaise and add to the crabmeat mixture.

The sandwich fillings should be covered with lettuce leaves, watercress, or shredded green or red cabbage before being covered.

When interviewing a new sandwich boy, look at his hands to see if he is inclined to be nervous.

Cream Cheese and Almond Spread

YIELDS 1 CUP

1/2 pound cream cheese
2 tablespoons pickle relish
4 tablespoons chopped almonds

2 tablespoons chopped celery
Salt and pepper to taste
Paprika
Worcestershire sauce

Combine the cream cheese, relish, almonds, and celery. Season to taste with salt, pepper, and paprika. Add a dash of Worcestershire sauce.

Egg Spread

YIELDS 2/3 CUP

2 eggs, hard-boiled, chopped

1 tablespoon mustard or chili sauce

Combine the eggs with mustard or chili sauce.

Grated Cheese and Walnut Spread

YIELDS ¾ CUP

¾ cup grated Swiss cheese
⅓ cup minced walnuts

2 tablespoons mayonnaise
1 tablespoon mustard

Blend the cheese with the walnuts and the mayonnaise with the mustard. Combine the two.

Ham Spread

YIELDS 1 CUP

¾ cup chopped ham
1 tablespoon chopped pickles
1½ tablespoons chopped olives
2 tablespoons minced parsley

1½ tablespoons chopped onion
1½ tablespoons mayonnaise
Salt
Pepper

Combine the ham, pickles, olives, parsley, onion, and mayonnaise. Season to taste with salt and pepper.

*I*nspect fingernails every day. They must be kept short for handling food.

illings should be moist enough to chew easily yet not so moist that filling drips when the sandwich is eaten.

Liver and Bacon Spread

YIELDS 1¼ CUPS

1 cup chopped, cooked chicken livers

4 slices bacon, broiled crisp, chopped

1½ tablespoons catsup

Combine the livers, bacon, and catsup.

Roquefort Cheese Spread

YIELDS 1 SERVING

1½ tablespoons Roquefort cheese

1½ tablespoons cream cheese

Worcestershire sauce

1½ tablespoons chopped walnuts

Cream the Roquefort and cream cheese together. Season with Worcestershire sauce and mix in the walnuts.

Sandwiches

Cutting the meat approximately the same size as the bread speeds up service and does away with tearing off corners.

Women prefer a moist sandwich while men will eat a crunchy sandwich. Men will take a three-decker and women prefer a single.

Spicy Ham Filling

YIELDS 2 CUPS

1 cup minced ham
1/3 cup minced pickles
1/3 cup minced black olives
1 tablespoon minced parsley
1 tablespoon minced onion

1 tablespoon minced pimiento
2 teaspoons brown sugar
1/2 teaspoon dry mustard
Salt and pepper to taste
Mayonnaise

Combine all of the ingredients and moisten with mayonnaise.

Spicy Savory Filling

YIELDS 1 CUP

1/2 cup chopped, cooked bacon
1/2 cup peanut butter
2 teaspoons Worcestershire sauce

Pinch of curry powder
Catsup

Combine the first four ingredients and moisten with catsup.

Tuna Fish Spread

YIELDS 1 CUP

1 teaspoon curry powder 1 cup shredded tuna fish
4 tablespoons mayonnaise

Blend the curry powder with the mayonnaise and combine with the tuna.

TOASTS

*T*hough we think of toasts today in terms of breakfast foods like French toast, toasts were a popular item at the soda fountain all day long. They were consumed as breakfast, lunch, or a light snack, and they varied from the richness of butterscotch toast to the stomach-calming austerity of milk toast (also known as "Graveyard Stew"). In re-creating these toasts, use fresh, unsliced bread if possible and slice it into thick half-inch slabs so that the outside remains crisp when toasted and the inside soft.

From just the ordinary everyday ingredients that you have always on hand, you can produce, almost magically, a truly delightful toast.

*n*ew creations tempt jaded palates.

Baltimore Toast

SERVES 3

1 egg, beaten
1 cup milk
¼ cup sugar
1 teaspoon cinnamon

6 slices white bread
Flour
Butter

Mix the beaten egg with the milk and stir in the sugar and cinnamon. Dip each slice of bread into the egg mixture and then into flour. Fry in butter. Serve hot with jelly or jam.

Banana Cinnamon Toast

SERVES 1

2 slices white bread,
    toasted
Butter

2 bananas, sliced
Cinnamon

Cut the crusts from the toast. Butter lightly and cut into 2 triangles. Arrange the banana slices on the toast, sprinkle lightly with cinnamon, and place under the broiler for 1 or 2 minutes.

Butterscotch Toast

SERVES 1

2 slices white bread, crusts
   removed
Butter, creamed

Brown sugar
Cinnamon

Cut bread into triangles and toast on one side. Spread the untoasted side with a mixture of creamed butter and brown sugar. Broil until the mixture is hot and bubbly. Sprinkle with cinnamon.

Cheese Toast

SERVES 3

1/4 pound Swiss cheese
   Salt to taste
1/4 teaspoon mustard
1/2 teaspoon paprika
   Butter

1/2 egg
3/8 to 1/2 cup milk or stock,
   warmed
6 slices whole wheat
   bread, toasted

Preheat oven to 350° F. Cut the cheese into small pieces and mix with salt, mustard, and paprika. Place the mixture in a 1½-cup buttered ovenproof bowl. Beat the egg slightly, add it to the warm milk or stock, and pour over the cheese mixture. The liquid should barely cover the cheese. Bake 10 to 15 minutes, until the cheese is melted and a slightly brown crust has formed. Place the cheese on fresh toast. Cut into triangles or quarters and serve.

Sandwiches

The customer is a mighty exacting individual. He not only expects good food, but he demands it and must have it.

Cherry Toast

SERVES 1

¾ cup pitted chopped cherries

2 tablespoons cream

2 slices white bread, thickly cut

Heat the cherries in the cream over low heat. Cut the bread into thick fingers and toast in the oven so that they are brown on the outside and remain soft inside. Put the hot cherries into a dish and arrange the toast fingers over them. Serve with cream.

Florida Orange Toast

SERVES 1

¼ cup orange juice

1 orange rind, grated

½ cup sugar

2 slices white bread, toasted, buttered

Mix the orange juice, rind, and sugar. Spread on sizzling hot buttered toast. Brown under the broiler and serve at once.

French Applesauce Toast

SERVES 1

2 slices whole wheat
  bread, 1½-inches thick

Butter, melted
Applesauce, hot

Remove bread crusts and cut each slice into three strips, making oblong blocks. Toast on all sides, dip into melted butter, and roll in thick, hot applesauce. Serve at once.

Jelly Roll Toast

SERVES 1

2 slices day-old white
  bread

Jelly (your choice)

Cut the crusts from the bread and spread each slice with jelly. Roll up each slice and secure with a toothpick. Put the rolled slices seam-side down on a baking sheet and cover with a damp cloth until ready to serve. Toast under the broiler. Serve hot.

Do not use girls for sandwich work. They cut themselves and faint. Girls are not as fast. Speed is essential.

Milk Toast

SERVES 1

2 slices toast
Butter
1¼ to 1½ cups milk

Salt
White pepper
Paprika

Put the toast into a heated bowl. The toast may be buttered or not. Bring the milk to a boil and pour over the toast. Season with salt, white pepper, and paprika.

Water Toast

SERVES 1

2 slices white bread,
   toasted
Salt
Water

Butter
Watercress
Tomato slice

Dip very dry toast into boiling salted water. Spread with butter and serve immediately. Garnish with watercress and a slice of tomato.

ACKNOWLEDGMENTS

We would like to thank Sheryl Julian and Lisa Wagner for bringing the illustrator and editor together; Marge Leibenstein for introducing us to Anne Edelstein and Writers House; Sheila Tully for assistance in editing; Kathy Flynn, Anne Fraser, Taxia Cullen, Kathleen Fraser, and Martha Fraser for help in testing and tasting the recipes; and finally Erica Marcus, our editor at Crown, for seeing the possibilities of the book and carrying it through.

In memory of my father, Charles R. Vidinghoff, who made the best milk shakes.

INDEX

Index

Soda Fountain menu making consists largely of coming up with attractive plate combinations. Portion sizes can be small because most of the patronage is made up of women. Heavy eaters will go elsewhere. Standards of food preparation and service should be as high as in the better restaurants. Sanitation is essential — especially in dish washing.

If you operate your business by these standards you should show a profit of 10 to 20 percent of your gross sales.